INDOOR ACTIVITIES

Written & Illustrated by
Jennifer Walsh McIntosh

b.dazzle, inc.®
producers of gifts, games and fun

240 The Village, Suite 309, Redondo Beach, California 90277-2535

Kids on the *Go*™
Indoor Activities

Written & Illustrated
by
Jennifer Walsh McIntosh

Edited by
Kathleen Gavin & Marshall Gavin

© 1994 b. dazzle, inc.
Published by b. dazzle, inc.,
240 The Village, Suite 309, Redondo Beach, California 90277-2535
Telephone: 310-374-3000; Fax 310-318-6692

ISBN: 1-885437-03-X

b. dazzle, inc. Item #783350-40004

CONTENTS

INTRODUCTION

Turn indoor times into fun times with the games and projects in this book. Take this book with you when you travel out of town. It's terrific for birthday parties, overnights with friends or staying inside on rainy and bad weather days!

Personalize your book by coloring the pictures. Activities that are super quiet, appropriate for a restaurant or a waiting room for example, have a 👉 at the top of each page.

Most of the activities in this book require nothing more than people, pencils and paper. However, to get the most out of your time spent indoors, you may want to keep a travel bag stocked with other materials such as crayons, markers, colored paper, scissors, tape and a glue stick.

To all of you KIDS ON THE GO™, turn off that TV and tune in to active fun!

BALANCE THE BOOK

2 or more people • hardcover books

1.   Each person holds a book on his head and lines up against the wall.

2.   On the word, "Go!" each person drops his hands, balances the book and walks to the opposite wall.

3.   Each time someone drops a book, he has to start all over again from the wall.

4.   The first person to reach the opposite wall wins.

Variations:

• Make this easier by walking a shorter distance.

4

BALLOON BALL

2 or more people • balloon

1. Divide the room in half with a barrier, such as a line of chairs, a roll of blankets, a rope or a long piece of tape.

2. Divide the players into two teams with one team on one side of the barrier and the other team on the other side.

3. One team begins by tossing up the balloon and batting it over the barrier with their hands.

4. Each team has to keep the ball in the air when it's on their side. If it falls on the floor the other team gets a point.

5. The first team to reach 20 points wins.

BLIND MAN'S BLUFF

4 or more people • blindfold

1.   Put on the blindfold while the other players make a circle around you.

2.   Count to 20 while everyone walks around you. When you reach 20, stop counting and everyone stands still.

3.   Point your hand straight out in front of you. The player closest to your hand steps up beside you.

4.   Try to guess who he is by feeling his face.

5.   If you guess correctly, this person takes your place. If you guess incorrectly then take one more turn.

Variations:

• Try to guess the player's identity by listening to his voice instead of touching him.

8

CARD TOSS

2 to 4 people • cards • container
(trash basket, paper bag, hat, box, etc.)

1.   Separate the cards into suits and give each player a pile.

2.   Sit in a wide circle with the container in the middle.

3.   Each person takes a turn tossing his cards into the container.

4.   The cards that land in the container are added up as follows: 15 points for face cards and actual number values for the rest.

5.   The highest score wins.

CHARADES

4 or more people • paper • pencil • clock

1. Make two teams.

2. Pick a category of books, songs or movies.

3. *Team 1* secretly thinks of a title such as *Little Red Riding Hood* and whispers it to one person chosen from *Team 2.*

4. This person acts out the title to his own team word by word. No speaking allowed!

5. *Team 1* times *Team 2* and stops the clock when someone guesses the correct title.

6. Now it's *Team 2*'s turn to think up a name.

7. The team that guesses correctly in the least amount of time wins.

FAN BALL

2 people • paper

1.   Make fans by folding pieces of paper back and forth in 1/2" strips.

2.   Crumple a piece of paper into a ball and place it in the middle of a smooth topped table or a hard floor.

3.   Each person holds his fan and sits on either side of the crumpled paper ball.

4.   On the word, "Go!" each person tries to move the ball to the other person's side by fanning furiously. Touching the ball is not allowed!

5.   The person who succeeds in moving the ball to the other person's side, scores a point. Play up to a preset number of points. The winner is the highest scorer.

HOT POTATO

4 or more people • radio or recorded music

1.   Use a shoe or a ball for the hot potato. Or use a real potato (not a hot one, though) if available!

2.   One person turns on the music without looking at the other players. The rest of the players sit in a circle and pass the hot potato quickly around.

3.   When the music is suddenly turned off, the person left holding the hot potato drops out.

4.   Continue until one person remains.

INSTANT DRINKING CUP

1 or more persons • paper • scissors

1. Make any size piece of paper into a square by folding and cutting it like this:

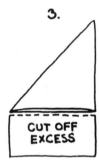

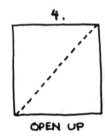

2. Fold it into a drinking cup by following the illustrations on the next page.

3. Open the cup up, fill it with water, and drink!

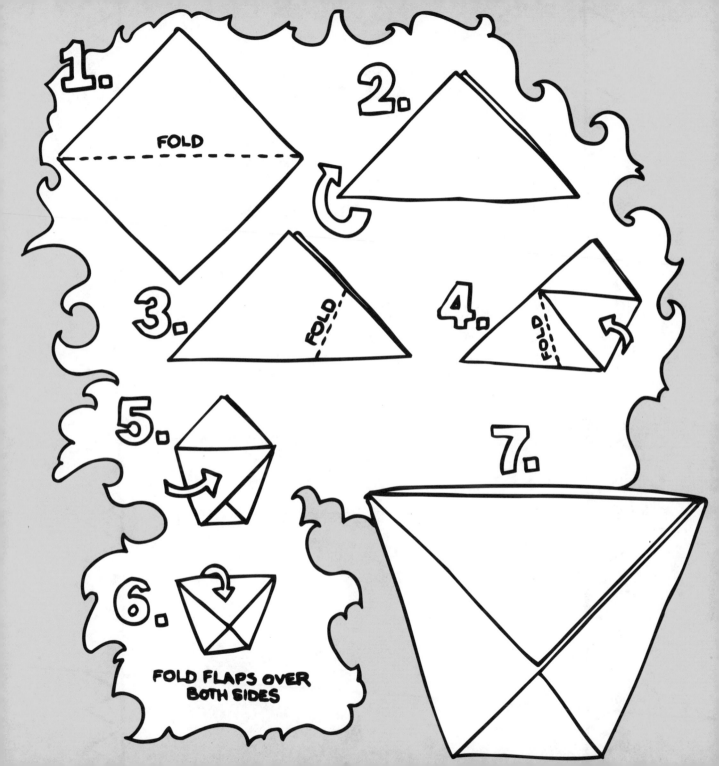

1.

FOLD

2.

3.

FOLD

4.

FOLD

5.

6.

FOLD FLAPS OVER
BOTH SIDES

7.

KICK BALL

2 or more people • newspaper

1. Each player crumples up a piece of newspaper into a ball.

2. Plan an indoor racing route. For example, in your house you could go around a chair, in and out of the bathroom, down the hall and back, then back to home base.

3. On the word, "Go!" each player kicks his ball around the route.

4. The winner is the first person to reach home base.

LEAPFROG

2 people

1.   Stand in front of your partner, squat down and put your hands on the floor for balance.

2.   Signal your partner when you're ready by croaking like a frog, "Ribbit, ribbit!"

3.   He puts his hands on your back, leaps over you and squats down in front, and tells you to jump by croaking too.

4.   Play leapfrog from room to room until you're all jumped out!

Variations:

• It's fun to have leapfrog races against other teams.

MEMORY

2 or more people • cards

1. Shuffle the cards and lay them face down in straight columns and rows.

2. Randomly turn two cards over. If they're pairs, keep them and take another turn. If they don't match, turn them over in the same place and it's the next person's turn.

3. The object is for each person to remember the position of each card that's turned over so that he can make a match on his next turn.

4. The winner is the person who collects the most pairs.

MOBIUS STRIP

1 or more persons • paper • pencil
• scissors • tape

1.   Cut a 2" wide strip from the long side of a piece of paper.

2.   Twist one end and then tape the two ends together.

3.   Draw a pencil line along the middle of the strip. Keep going until you reach the beginning of the line again. It's as if the strip has only one side!

4.   Cut the strip along the line. What happens?

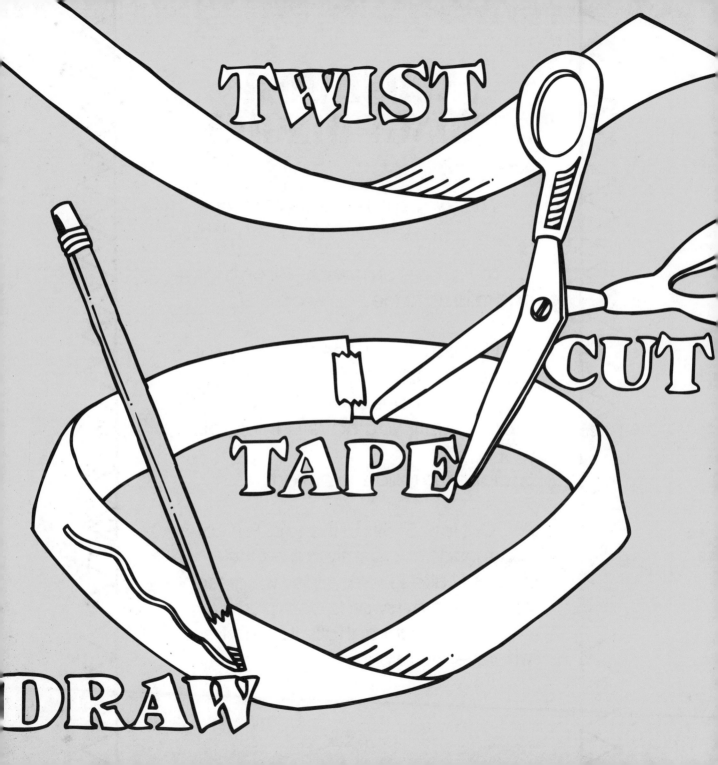

NEWSPAPER THINGY WINGIES

1 or more persons • newspaper • tape • scissors

1.   Lay a sheet of newspaper on a table and roll it up to the center crease.

2.   Place a second sheet over the flat part and roll this up to the center. Add 4 to 8 more sheets in the same manner until you have a thick roll.

3.   Tape the roll at the bottom.

4.   Cut four 5" slits in the top. Put your finger inside and gently pull out the insides. Make several *thingy wingies* and pretend they're swords, pom poms, decorations, animal tails, flowers, trees - whatever you wish!

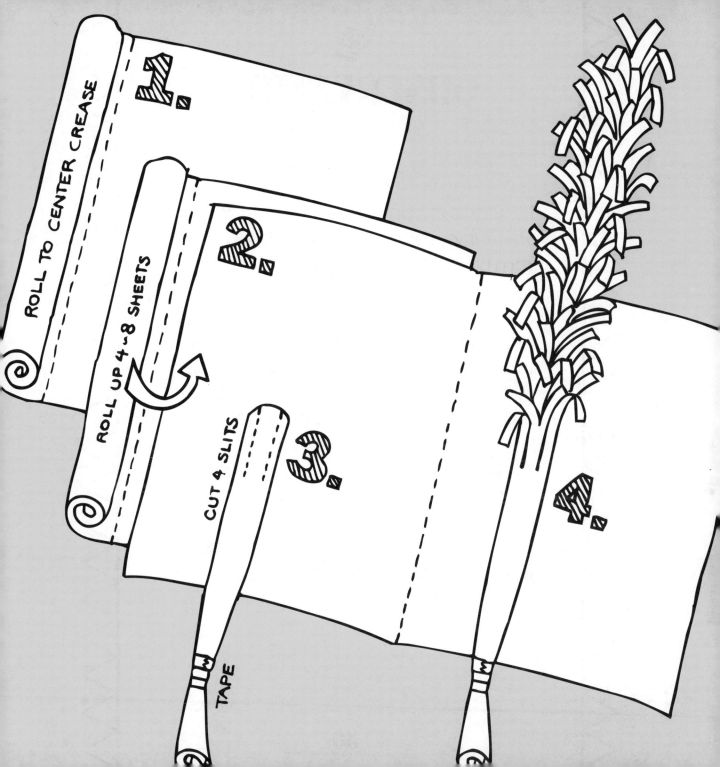

OBSERVATION

2 or more people

1. Stand in front of the other players for about thirty seconds as they observe you from head to toe. Then leave the room.

2. While you're out of sight, change something about your appearance. For example, untie a shoe, change the part in your hair, pull down one sock or make any other slight but visible change.

3. Return to the room and stand in front of the players again.

4. The first player to correctly guess what you've changed about yourself takes your turn.

PAPER BASKETBALL

1 or more persons • paper • wire coat hanger

1.   Bend the hanger into a half circle, and hook it over the top of a door.

2.   Scrunch the paper into tight balls. Give five paper balls to each person playing.

3.   Stand on the other side of the room, and take turns tossing the balls through the basket. (Younger players may stand a little closer.)

4.   Keep score to determine the winner.

Variations:

• If you don't have a wire hanger you can toss the paper balls into a small waste paper basket placed on top of a dresser. A paper bag, hat or shoe may also be used.

PAPER HAT

*1 or more persons • paper • ruler • tape
• crayons or markers*

1.   Tape pieces of paper together so that you end up with a 22" x 16" sheet.

2.   Make a paper hat by following the steps in the illustrations on the next page.

3.   Use crayons or markers to decorate the hat.

Variations:

• Cut out paper feathers or flowers and tape them to your hat.

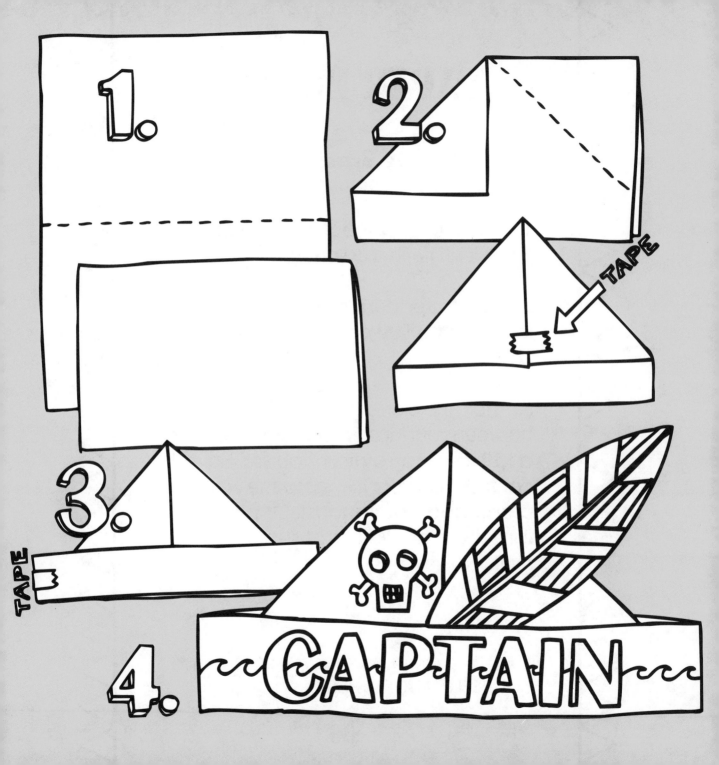

1.

2.

TAPE

3.

TAPE

4. CAPTAIN

PAPER PLANES

1 or more persons • paper • crayons or markers • tape

1.   Decorate a piece of paper (approx. 8 1/2" x 11") with a colorful design.

2.   Fold the paper into a plane by following the illustrations on the next page.

3.   Hold the plane at the bottom between your thumb and your forefinger, and throw* it away from yourself. Have contests with your friends to see whose plane goes the farthest. Or pick a target on the wall, and see who can hit it.

* ALWAYS AIM PLANES AWAY FROM YOURSELF AND OTHERS.

1.

2.

3.

4.

TAPE

PAPER SHUFFLE

2 or more people • paper

1.   Each person lines up against the wall with each foot on a piece of paper.

2.   On the word, "Go!" each player shuffles to the opposite wall without taking their feet off the paper.

3.   Players who step off the paper must start over.

4.   The person who reaches the opposite wall first wins.

PASS THE BALLOON

3 or more people • balloon

1.   Everyone stands in a circle.

2.   Blow up a balloon, knot it securely and tuck it under your chin.

3.   Pass it to the person next to you by tucking it under *his* chin - but without using your hands!

4.   See how many times the balloon can go around the circle without it popping or falling to the floor.

PUSH THE BALLOON

2 or more people • balloons

1. Each person blows up and knots his balloon.

2. Each player kneels down with his heels touching the wall behind him and his nose touching his balloon on the floor.

3. On the word, "Go!" each player crawls to the opposite wall while pushing the balloon in front of him with his nose. No hands allowed!

4. The first person to reach the opposite wall wins.

SHOE SHUFFLE

4 or more people • running shoes

1.   Everyone removes their shoes and mixes them together in a pile at the end of the room.

2.   The players line up against the opposite wall.

3.   On the word, "Go!" everyone races to the pile of shoes, finds their own, puts them on, ties up the laces then races back to the wall.

4.   The first person to reach the wall is the winner.

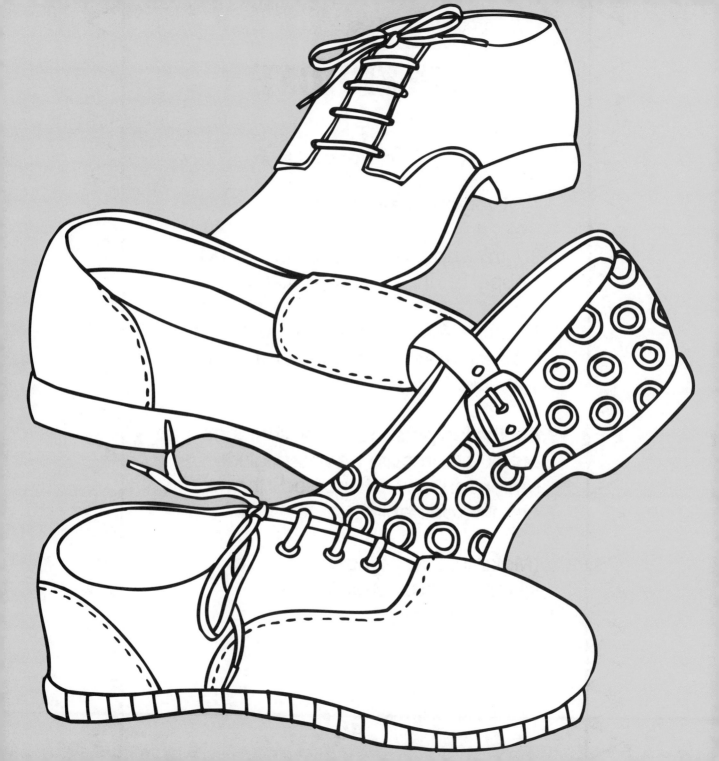

TELEPHONE

5 or more people

1.   Everyone sits in a circle.

2.   Think up a long, silly sentence and whisper it to the person on your right.

3.   That person whispers the sentence to the person on his right, and so on around the circle.

4.   The last person says the sentence out loud. Compare it to your original sentence. Don't be surprised if the two are quite different!

(Make sure everyone gets a turn at thinking up a sentence.)

25¢ WALK

2 or more people • quarters • tape

1.   Everyone lines up against the wall with a quarter and a piece of tape.

2.   On the word, "Go!" the players tip back their heads, tape the quarters to their foreheads and walk quickly to the opposite wall.

3.   Players who drop their quarters must start again.

4.   The first person to reach the wall wins.

Variations:

• You may try this without the tape to make things more challenging!

WET, DRY OR DOES IT FLY?

3 or more people

1.   Think of an animal that is *wet* (living in water), *dry* (living on land), or an animal that *flies.*

2.   Ask, "Wet, dry or does it fly?" Point to someone and say one of the categories, for example, "Wet!"

3.   Count to ten quickly while this person names an animal. The answers must be specific such as "Rainbow Trout!"

4.   If you count to ten before the other person thinks of an animal then it's your turn again. If he says an animal before you reach ten, then it's his turn.

WHEN I'M BIG

2 or more people

1.   Start by saying, "When I'm big, I want to be a . . . " Finish your thought by acting the part of an adult doing his job. Some people to imitate are teachers, truck drivers, farmers, cooks, doctors, mothers, dancers, artists, baseball players, fathers, pianists, hockey players, etc.

2.   The other players take turns guessing who you are.

3.   Make sure everyone gets a turn at acting.

Look For These Other High Value Educational Activities from

b.dazzle, inc.®
producers of gifts, games and fun

Color 'n Seek®

Create An Original Work of Art While Discovering A World Of Hidden Images.
Be fascinated for hours by the challenge of coloring the poster's picture and seeking the images hidden within the overall Color 'n Seek® design.

SCRAMBLE SQUARES®

Easy to Play, But Hard To Solve.

Challenging educational puzzles with powerful graphics on nine 4" x 4" squares that will keep girls, boys, and adults captivated for hours! Each of the many collectible Scramble Squares® titles includes facts and a trivia quiz on its subject.

COLOR MY TOWN™

Real Estate Has Never Been So Affordable!

Activity Sets to color, sticker and stimulate the imagination.